William Henry Corrie Kerr

The Heroides of Ovid

Epistles I. and XIII.

William Henry Corrie Kerr

The Heroides of Ovid
Epistles I. and XIII.

ISBN/EAN: 9783337194864

Printed in Europe, USA, Canada, Australia, Japan

Cover: Foto ©ninafisch / pixelio.de

More available books at **www.hansebooks.com**

THE HEROIDES

OF

OVID.

[EPISTLES I. AND XIII.]

WITH NOTES,

BY

WILLIAM H. C. KERR, M. A.

TORONTO:
ROLLO & ADAM.
1865.

PREFACE.

———◆———

THIS little work will be of some use to the Boys of the Grammar Schools of Upper Canada, who intend to Matriculate at the Junior Matriculation Examination in the University of Toronto. The text is, with but few alterations, the Eton text. To notes carefully selected from Burmann, Loers, Cookesley, Browne, Bentley and Lemaire, I have added many of my own. The young student will find the best notes on the Heroides in Andrew's Latin Lexicon, Smith's Classical Dictionary, and Schmitz's Latin Grammar, to which his attention is earnestly directed by

THE EDITOR.

LIFE OF OVID.

—

His Birth.

Publius Ovidius Naso was born at Sulmo (*Sulmone*), a town of the Peligni (*Abruzzi*), ninety miles distant from Rome, on the 20th March, B.C. 43 : the year in which the consuls Hirtius and Pansa fell in the field of Mutina (*Modena*). His family was of the Equestrian Order.

His Education.

While still young, he, with his brother Lucius, who was exactly a year older than himself, was sent to Rome to receive their education. Lucius was destined for the bar, but died at the early age of twenty. Ovid studied rhetoric under Arellius Fuscus and Porcius Latro, but the indolent boy spent the hours which he should have devoted to jurisprudence in writing love-songs and fugitive pieces of poetry. Ovid's father discouraged the cultivation of his poetical talents, as tending to poverty ; but all in vain. The full though easy flowing current of his genius would find vent in numbers, whenever he tried to write plain prose. Having completed his education at Athens, he travelled with the poet Macer in Asia and Sicily.

His Civil Offices.

When he assumed the *toga. virilis*, it was bordered with a broad purple stripe—the badge of the patrician order ; but, being unambitious and indolent, he never took his seat in the senate. He filled, however, several magisterial and judicial offices, having been made one of the *Triumviri Capitales*, and subsequently one of the *Decemviri*, who presided over the *Centumviri*—a court for the trial of testamentary and criminal causes.

His Contemporaries.

His rank, fortune, and talents, enabled him to cultivate the acquaintance of the best poets of his day. Macer and Propertius would recite their compositions to him; Ponticus and Bassus were guests at his table. He had heard the lyrics of Horace read by himself. Virgil he had only seen; and the untimely death of Tibullus prevented him from making the acquaintance of that poet. Among the minor poets of the Ovidian age, we may mention Gratius Faliscus, a writer of harsh heroics; Pedo Albinovauus, an epic poet, and the trusty friend of Ovid; M. Manilius, a philosophical poet; and A. Sabinus, who wrote answers to six of the Epistles of the Heroides, none of which are extant.

His Character.

Epicurean in his tastes, and a skeptic, if not a disbeliever in a future state, Ovid lived a life of continual self-indulgence and intrigue. He himself confesses his natural susceptibility and amorous temperament. Popular as a poet, and successful in society, he possessed all the enjoyments which wealth could bestow. He was a universal admirer of, and as universal a favorite with, the female sex, in the voluptuous capital. He married twice in early life, at the desire of his parents, but he speedily divorced each of his wives in succession. From his third wife, whom he sincerely loved, and by whom he had a daughter, Perilla, he was only separated by

His Exile.

After enjoying the friendship of a large circle of distinguished men, and the favour of Augustus himself, in A,D. 9, Ovid was suddenly commanded by an imperial edict to transport himself to Tomi (*Tomoswar*), a town on the Euxine, near the moûth of the Danube, in the marshy, barren country of the rude and uncivilized Getæ. The sole reason assigned in the edict for his banishment was his having published his poem on the Art of Love. The real cause is suspected to have been some intrigue with one of the members of the imperial family, but the whole affair is involved in obscurity. Whatever may have been the cause, the punishment was a cruel one. Ovid, who, with all his faults, was affectionate and tender-hearted, was torn from all the voluptuous blandishments of the capital, from the sympathies of congenial spirits, who could appreciate his talents, and from the arms of his weeping wife, and was hurried off in the depth of winter, without any preparations for his voyage, to an abode as inhospitable and inclement as that of Scythia. He lived in exile only ten years; constant anxiety preyed upon his bodily health, and, after a lingering illness, he died in the sixtieth year of his age, A.D. 18. The Tomitæ shewed their respect by erecting a tomb to his memory.

His Works.

All the extant poems of Ovid, with the exception of the Metamorphoses, are elegiac. It was the metre then most in vogue. His principal works are, 1, *Amorum Libri* III.; 2, *Epistolæ Heroidum*, twenty-one in number; 3, *Ars Amatoria;* 4, *Remedia Amoris;* 5, *Metamorphoseon Libri* XV.; 6, *Fastorum Libri* XII.; 7, *Tristium Libri* V.; 8, *Epistolarum Ex Ponto Libri* IV. His minor poems consist of the *Medea,* a lost tragedy; *Ibis,* a satire; *Nux,* an elegy; and some fragments on Cosmetics and Fishing.

CHRONOLOGICAL TABLE.

B. C.	LITERARY CHRONOLOGY.	CIVIL CHRONOLOGY.
43	Birth of Ovid; Death of Cicero.	Second triumvirate formed.
42	Horace at Philippi.	
34	Death of Sallust.	
31	Virgil, (born B. C. 70); Mæcenas; Horace; Varius; Tibullus; Cornelius Gallus and Plotius Tucca.	Battle of Actium.
25	Propertius; Ovid; A. Sabinus; Livy; Macer; Ateius Capito and Vitruvius.	
19	Death of Virgil.	
18	Death of Tibullus.	
17	Carmen Sæculare of Horace.	Ludi Sæculares.
8	Death of Horace.	
4		BIRTH OF OUR LORD JESUS CHRIST.
A.D.		
9	Exile of Ovid.	Defeat of Quintilius Varus.
14		Death of Augustus.
18	Deaths of Ovid and Livy; Valerius Maximus; C. Asinius Gallus.	Sejanus the imperial favorite.

ON ELEGIAC VERSE.

(*From Dr. McCaul's " Course of Classical Study.*")

" In the Elegiac distich, Ovid of course must be your model for Latin, as Tyrtæus, Theognis, Euripides, or Callimachus, for Greek. The Latin pentameter is regulated by severe laws. The cæsural division must not be violated by elision, although Catullus might be quoted as authority for the license. The first penthemimer should not terminate with a spondee followed by a monosyllable ; nor should a monosyllable close the verse, except with elision. You may regard it as a general rule, that the final word must be dissyllabic. The only exception which can be permitted is in the case of a quadrisyllable. An adverb should rarely appear in the last place ; a present participle almost never. The sense, also, must not overflow from one couplet into another ; or, if it should, the only termination for it is the end of the second."

SCALES OF THE METRE.

I. The *Dactylic Hexameter* consists, as its name imports, of six feet ; in the first four places, dactyls or spondees may be used at pleasure ; the fifth foot is usually a dactyl, the sixth invariably a spondee, as represented in the following scheme :

$$ -\cup\cup \mid -\cup\cup \mid -\cup\cup \mid -\cup\cup \mid -\cup\cup \mid \quad\cup $$
$$ -- \mid\quad -- \mid\quad -- \mid\quad -- \mid [--] \mid -- $$

II. The *Dactylic Pentameter* is composed of two *Dactylic Penthemimers*, or, in other words, two *Dactylic Trimeters Catalectic* joined together. The first two feet may be either dactyls or spondees ; they are followed by a cæsural syllable, then two dactyls, and another cæsural syllable, thus :—

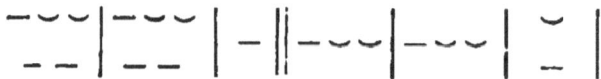

$$ -\smile\smile \mid -\smile\smile \mid \ -\parallel -\smile\smile \mid -\smile\smile \mid \ \smile \mid $$
$$ -\ - \mid -\ - \mid \qquad\qquad \ - \mid $$

The melody of Ovid's hexameters is in a great measure owing to his careful attention to the Cæsura. He is also very careful in the choice and arrangement of the closing words of each line, which greatly contributes to the smoothness of the rhythm. But it is in the artistic and graceful structure of his pentameters that Ovid far surpasses the Greeks and their imitators, Catullus, Tibullus, and Propertius. With him, the first Cæsura always is the last syllable of a word, and the last word of the line nearly always a dissyllable. We occasionally find *est* in this latter place, preceded by a dissyllable which suffers elision. Of these we have three instances in these two Epistles : (Ep. I. 20, Ep. XIII. 76 and 112).

This species of verse received the name *Elegiac* from its having been originally employed in mournful strains. Its province was, however, in process of time, much extended. It was used by the Greeks in hymns, epigrams, and even war songs : and by the Romans in epigrams, epistles, and all kinds of amatory poetry.

P. OVIDII NASONIS HEROIDUM

EPIST. I.

PENELOPE ULYSSI.

ARGUMENT.

Ulysses, king of Ithaca, was one of the most famous of the Greek chieftains who took part in the expedition against Troy. At the end of the war, he set out on his return home ; but for ten years was driven about to various parts of the Mediterranean Sea. He met with a great variety of adventures, and visited various strange countries. His wife Penelope, in the meanwhile, being filled with anxiety and perplexity, in consequence of hearing no tidings of him, writes him this letter. She begins by entreating him to return, and curses the day on which Paris sailed to Lacedæmon (vv. 1-6). Whilst Troy was standing, she was always fancying her husband would be killed (vv. 11-22): but when Troy was destroyed, all the chieftains returned home, and charmed their wives by stories of the brave deeds of their countrymen. In this way Penelope had heard of the deeds of Ulysses himself : for she had sent her son Telemachus to Pylus, and there he talked with Nestor (vv. 25-45). But what was the use to her of Troy having been taken, if Ulysses did not return home ? Nay, it would be better, as far as she was concerned, if Troy were still standing; for at any rate she would know where her husband was (*vv.* 47–70). She does not know exactly what to fear; but she fears everything. Possibly he may have fallen in love with some other person! (*vv.* 71–80). Meanwhile, her own father Icarius, taking for granted that Ulysses must be dead, is constantly urging her to marry some one else. The chieftains of the neighbouring islands are all wooing her, and plundering the kingdom of Ulysses (*vv.* 81–94). Even the beggar Irus and the herdsman Melanthius insult her. She has no one to protect her but Laertes, the aged father, and Telemachus, the youthful son, of Ulysses. Out of reverence for his father, and in order that he may be the defender of his son, Ulysses ought to return (*v.* 95, *ad fin.*)

HANC tua Penelope lento tibi mittit, Ulysse :
Nil mihi rescribas ; attamen ipse veni.
Troja jacet certe, Danais invisa puellis :
Vix Priamus tanti, totaque Troja, fuit.
5 O utinam tunc, cum Lacedæmona classe petebat,
Obrutus insanis esset adulter aquis !
Non ego deserto jacuissem frigida lecto,
Nec quererer tardos ire relicta dies :
Nec mihi, quærenti spatiosam fallere noctem,
10 Lassaret viduas pendula tela manus.
Quando ego non timui graviora pericula veris ?
Res est solliciti plena timoris amor.
In te fingebam violentos Troas ituros :
Nomine in Hectoreo pallida semper eram.
15 Sive quis Antilochum narrabat ab Hectore victum,
Antilochus nostri causa timoris erat :

Sive Menœtiaden falsis cecidisse sub armis,
   Flebam successu posse carere dolos.
Sanguine Tlepolemus Lyciam tepefecerat hastam ;
20   Tlepolemi leto cura novata mea est.
Denique, quisquis erat castris jugulatus Achivis,
   Frigidius glacie pectus amantis erat.
Sed bene consuluit casto deus æquus amori ;
   Versa est in cinerem sospite Troja viro.
25 Argolici rediere duces ; altaria fumant ;
   Ponitur ad patrios barbara præda deos.
Grata ferunt nymphæ pro salvis dona maritis ;
   Illi victa suis Troia fata canunt.
Mirantur justique senes, trepidæque puellæ ;
30   Narrantis conjux pendet ab ore viri.
Atque aliquis posita monstrat fera prælia mensa ;
   Pingit et exiguo Pergama tota mero :
" Hac ibat Simoïs ; hic est Sigeïa tellus ;
   Hic steterat Priami regia celsa senis.
35 Illic Æacides, illic tendebat Ulysses ;
   Hic lacer admissos terruit Hector equos."
Omnia namque tuo senior, te quærere misso,
   Rettulerat nato Nestor ; at ille mihi.
Rettulit et ferro Rhesumque Dolonaque cæsos ;
40   Utque sit hic somno proditus, ille dolo.
Ausus es, o nimium nimiumque oblite tuorum,
   Thracia nocturno tangere castra dolo ;
Totque simul mactare viros, adjutus ab uno !
   At bene cautus eras, et memor ante mei !
45 Usque metu micuere sinus ; dum victor amicum
   Dictus es Ismariis isse per agmen equis.

Sed mihi quid prodest vestris disjecta lacertis
  Ilios ? et, murus quod fuit ante, solum ?
Si maneo, qualis Troja durante manebam :
  Virque mihi, dempto fine carendus, abes ?
Diruta sunt aliis, uni mihi Pergama restant ;
  Incola captivo quæ bove victor arat.
Jam seges est, ubi Troja fuit ; resecandaque falce
  Luxuriat, Phrygio sanguine pinguis, humus.
Semisepulta virûm curvis feriuntur aratris
  Ossa : ruinosas occulit herba domos.
Victor abes ; nec scire mihi, quæ causa morandi,
  Aut in quo lateas ferreus orbe, licet.
Quisquis ad hæc vertit peregrinam littora puppim,
  Ille mihi de te multa rogatus abit.
Quamque tibi reddat, si te modo viderit usquam,
  Traditur huic digitis charta notata meis.
Nos Pylon, antiqui Neleïa Nestoris arva,
  Misimus : incerta est fama remissa Pylo.
Misimus et Sparten ; Sparte quoque nescia veri,
  Quas habitas terras, aut ubi lentus abes.
Utilius starent etiam nunc mœnia Phœbi ;
  (Irascor votis heu levis ipsa meis !)
Scirem, ubi pugnares ; et tantum bella timerem ;
  Et mea cum multis juncta querela foret.
Quid timeam ignoro ; timeo tamen omnia demens :
  Et patet in curas area lata meas.
Quæcunque æquor habet, quæcunque pericula tellus,
  Tam longæ causas suspicor esse moræ.
Hæc ego dum stulte meditor (quæ vestra libido est,)
  Esse peregrino captus amore potes.

Forsitan et narres, quam·sit tibi·rustica-conjux :
Quæ tantum lanas·non sinat' esse rudes.
Fallar ; et hoc·crimen tenues vanescat in auras :
80   Neve, revertendi liber, abesse velis.
Me pater Icarius viduo discedere lecto
Cogit, et immensas increpat usque moras.
Increpet usque licet ; tua·sum ; tua dicar oportet :
Penelope conjux semper Ulyssis ero.
85 Ille tamen pietate mea precibusque pudicis
Frangitur, et vires temperat ipse suas.
Dulichii, Samiique, et quos tulit alta Zacynthos,
Turba ruunt in me luxuriosa. proci ;
Inque tua regnant, nullis prohibentibus, aula :
90 Viscera nostra, tuæ dilaniantur opes.   [dirum,
Quid tibi. Pisandrum, Polybumque, Medontaque
Eurymachique avidas Antinoique manus,
Atque alios referam, quos omnes·turpiter absens
Ipse tuo partis sanguine rebus alis ?
95 Irus egens, pecorisque Melanthius actor edendi,
Ultimus accedunt in tua damna pudor.
Tres sumus imbelles numero ; sine viribus uxor,
Laërtesque senex, Telemachusque puer.
Ille per insidias pæne est mihi nuper ademptus,
100 Dum parat, invitis omnibus, ire Pylon.
Di, precor, hoc jubeant, ut, euntibus ordine fatis,
Ille meos oculos comprimat, ille tuos.
Hoc faciunt custosque boum, longævaque nutrix ;
Tertius, immundæ cura fidelis haræ.
105 Sed neque Laërtes, ut qui sit inutilis armis,
Hostibus in mediis regna tenere valet.

Telemacho veniet (vivat modo) fortior ætas :
Nunc erat auxiliis illa tuenda patris.
Nec mihi sunt vires inimicos pellere tectis.
110   Tu citius venias, portus et ara tuis !
Est tibi, sitque, precor, natus ; qui mollibus annis
In patrias artes erudiendus erat.
Respice Laërten : ut jam sua lumina condas,
Extremum fati sustinet ille diem.
115 Certe ego, quæ fueram, te discedente, puella,
Protinus ut redeas, facta videbor anus.

P. OVIDII NASONIS HEROIDUM

Epist. XIII.

—

LAODAMIA PROTESILAO.

—

ARGUMENT.

When the Greeks, under king Agamemnon, had resolved on making their famous expedition against Troy, they collected their forces and ships at Aulis, a town of Bœotia. The winds proving contrary, they were detained there for some time.

There was in the army a Thessalian, named Protesilaus. His wife Laodamia, hearing of the delay, wrote this letter to him; in which she tells him how much bitter grief she had suffered when he left her; how she stood upon the sea-shore, and strained her eyes in endeavouring to follow his ship, as he sailed away; and how, when she could see neither himself nor his vessel, she swooned away (*vv.* 17–24). She utters bitter reproaches against the wicked Paris, whose beauty was the curse and ruin of his country (*v.* 43). She cannot avoid giving expression to her feelings of terror: she has heard of Troy, and of one Hector, of whom she especially bids Protesilaus beware (*vv.* 51–66). Alas! she had good reason to dread Hector, for her husband was afterwards killed by him.

.   B

She fears Protesilaus is not destined to return home, for, as
he left his home his foot stumbled on the threshold (*vv.* 81–88).
She had been told that whoever was the first to land on the
Trojan shore, was doomed to be killed ; and she bids her husband take care that his ship was the last of all the fleet, and
that he was the last of his crew to land from it (*vv.* 89–94).
Having terrified herself by her own fancies, she imagines that
she sees the ghost of her dead husband. In an agony of grief
and dismay, she offers sacrifice to the deities of night (*vv.* 99–
104). She is alarmed by the fact that the Greeks are resolved
on leaving their native land, though the winds are contrary
(*vv.* 105–112). And she ends her letter by entreating Protesilaus, if he has any love for her, to take care of himself.

     Mittit, et optat amans quo mittitur ire, salutem,
       Hæmonis Hæmonio Laodamia viro.
     Aulide te fama est, vento retinente, morari—
       Ah ! me cum fugeres, hic ubi ventus erat ?
5   Tum freta debuerant vestris obsistere remis ;
       Illud erat sævis utile tempus aquis.
     Oscula plura viro, mandataque plura dedissem ;
       Et sunt quæ volui dicere plura tibi.
     Raptus es hinc præceps ; et, qui tua vela vocaret,
10   Quem cuperent nautæ, non ego, ventus erat.
     Ventus erat nautis aptus, non aptus amanti.
       Solvor ab amplexu, Protesilaë, tuo :
     Linguaque mandantis verba imperfecta relinquit ;
       Vix illud potui dicere triste, *Vale.*
15   Incubuit Boreas, abreptaque vela tetendit ;
       Jamque meus longe Protesilaüs erat.
     Dum potui spectare virum, spectare juvabat ;

Sumque tuos oculos usque secuta meis.
Ut te non poteram, poteram tua vela videre ;
20   Vela diu vultus detinuere meos.
At postquam nec te, nec vela fugacia vidi,
    Et quod spectarem, nil nisi pontus erat ;   ⁻.
Lux quoque tecum abiit, tenebrisque exsanguis
    obortis
Succiduo dicor procubuisse genu.
25 Vix socer Iphiclus, vix me grandævus Acastus,
    Vix mater gelida mœsta refecit aqua.
Officium fecere pium, sed inutile nobis :
    Indignor miseræ non licuisse mori.
Ut rediit animus, pariter rediere dolores ;
30   Pectora legitimus casta momordit amor.
Nec mihi pectendos cura est præbere capillos ;
    Nec libet aurata corpora veste tegi.
Ut quas pampinea tetigisse Bicorniger hasta
    Creditur ; huc illuc, quo furor egit, eo.
35 Conveniunt matres Phylaceïdes ; et mihi clamant,
    Indue regales, Laodamia, sinus.
Scilicet ipsa geram saturatas murice vestes,
    Bella sub Iliacis mœnibus ille gerat ?
Ipsa comas pectar ; galea caput ille prematur ?
40   Ipsa novas vestes, dura vir arma ferat ?
Qua possum, squalore tuos imitata labores
    Dicar ; et hæc belli tempora tristis agam.
Dyspari Priamide, damno formose tuorum,
    Tam sis hostis iners, quam malus hospes eras. ˙
45 Aut te Tænariæ faciem culpâsse maritæ,
    Aut illi vellem displicuisse tuam.

Tu, qui pro rapta nimium, Menelaë, laboras,
 Hei mihi ! quam multis flebilis ultor eris !
Dî, precor, a nobis omen removete sinistrum,
50 Et sua det reduci vir meus arma Jovi.
Sed timeo ; quotiesque subit miserabile bellum,
 More nivis lacrymæ, sole madentis, eunt.
Ilion et Tenedos Simoïsque et Xanthus et Ide,
 Nomina sunt ipso pæne timenda sono.
55 Nec rapere ausurus, nisi se defendere posset,
 Hospes erat : vires noverat ille suas.
Venerat (ut fama est) multo spectabilis auro,
 Quique suo Phrygias corpore ferret opes.
Classe virisque potens, per quæ fera bella geruntur,
60 Et sequitur regni pars quotacunque sui.
His ego te victam, consors Ledæa gemellis,
 Suspicor : hæc Danais posse nocere puto.
Hectora nescio quem timeo. Paris Hectora dixit
 Ferrea sanguinea bella movere manu.
65 Hectora, quisquis is est, si sum tibi cara, caveto :
 Signatum memori pectore nomen habe.
Hunc ubi vitâris, alios vitare memento ;
 Et multos illic Hectoras esse puta.
Et facito dicas, quoties pugnare parabis,
70 *Parcere me jussit Laodamia sibi.*
Si cadere Argolico fas est sub milite Trojam,
 Te quoque non ullum vulnus habente, cadat.
Pugnet, èt adversos tendat Menelaüs in hostes ;
 Ut rapiat Paridi, quam Paris ante sibi.
75 Irruat ; et causa quem vincit, vincat et armis.
 Hostibus e mediis nupta petenda viro est.

Causa tua est dispar.   Tu tantum vivere pugna,
Inque pios dominæ posse redire sinus.
Parcite, Dardanidæ, de tot (precor) hostibus uni,
80   Ne meus ex illo corpore sauguis eat.
Nunc fateor, volui revocare ; animusque ferebat :
Substitit auspicii lingua timoro mali.
Cum foribus velles ad Trojam exire paternis,
Pes tuus offcnso limine signa dedit.
85 Ut vidi, ingemui : tacitoque in pectore dixi :
Signa reversuri sint, precor, ista viri.
Hæc tibi nunc refero, ne sis animosus in armis :
Fac meus in ventos hic timor omnis eat.
Sors quoque nescio quem fato designat iniquo,
90   Qui primus Danaûm Troada tangat humum.
 · Infelix, quæ prima virum lugebit ademptum !
Di faciant, ne tu strcnuus esse velis !
Inter mille rates tua sit millesima puppis,
Jamque fatigatas ultima verset aquas.
95 Hoc quoque præmoneo ; de nave novissimus exi.
Non est, quo properes, terra paterna tibi.
Cum venies, remoque move veloque carinam :
Inque tuo celerem littorc siste gradum.
Sed tua cur nobis pallens occurrit imago ?
100   Cur venit a verbis multa querela tuis ?
Excutior somno ; simulacraque noctis adoro :
Nulla caret fumo Thessalis ara meo.
Thura damus, lacrymamque super ; qua sparsa re-
    lucet,
Ut solet adfuso surgcre flamma mero. ↲
105 Hoc quoque, quod venti prohibcnt exire carinas,

Me movet ; invitis ire paratis aquis.
Quis velit in patriam, vento prohibente, reverti ?
A patria pelago vela vetante datis.
Ipse suam non præbct iter Neptunus ad urbem :
110   Quo ruitis ? Vestras quisque redite domos.
Quo ruitis, Danai ? Ventos audite vetantes :
Non subiti casus, numinis ista mora est.
Quid petitur tanto, nisi turpis adultera, bello ?
Dum licet, Inachiæ, vertite vela, rates.
115 Sed quid ego revoco hæc ? Omen revocantis abesto ;
Blandaque compositas aura secundet aquas !
Ultima mandato claudetur epistola parvo !
"Si tibi cura mei, sit tibi cura tui."

NOTES.

Heroides.—Ovid calls these Epistles by this name because they are for the most part written by heroines : " *Heroinæ* "— the consorts of heroes.

The twenty-one *Epistolæ Heroidum* are a series of love-letters. Their characteristic feature is passion ; the ardour of which is sometimes interfered with by too laboured conceits and excessive refinement. They are, in fact, the most polished efforts of one whose natural indolence often disinclined him from expending that time and pains on the work of amending and correcting which distinguished Virgil. Their great merit consists in the remarkable neatness with which the sentiments are expressed, and the sweetness of the versification ; their great defect is want of variety. The subject necessarily limited the topics. The range of them is confined to laments for the absence of the beloved object, the pangs of jealousy, apprehensions of inconstancy, expressions of warm affection, and descriptions of the joys and sorrows of love.

Penelope was the daughter of Icarius and Peribœa of Sparta, and wife of Ulysses, by whom she had an only child, Telemachus, who was an infant when her husband sailed against Troy. During the long absence of Ulysses, she was beleaguered by numerous and importunate suitors, whom she deceived by declaring that she must finish a large robe for Laertes, her father-in-law, before she could make up her mind. During the day time, accordingly, she worked at the robe, and in the night undid the work of the day. By this means she succeeded in putting off the suitors. But her stratagem was at last betrayed by the servants; and when, in consequence, the faithful Penelope was pressed more and more by the impatient suitors, Ulysses at length arrived in Ithaca, after an absence of twenty years. Having recognized her husband by several signs, she heartily welcomed him, and the days of her grief and sorrow were at an end.

Ulyssi.—Ulysses, the son of Laertes (some say Sisyphus) and Anticlea, was early in life distinguished for courage, for knowledge of navigation, for eloquence, and for skill as a negotiator. It was with great difficulty he was prevailed upon to join the Greeks in their expedition against Troy. When Palamedes came on behalf of the confederates to invoke his aid, he pretended to be mad, and, having yoked an ass and an ox to a plough, began to sow salt. Palamedes, to try him, placed the infant Telemachus before the plough, whereupon the trick was discovered. Ulysses joined the Grecian fleet at Aulis with twelve ships, and during the siege of Troy distinguished himself as a valiant warrior, but more particularly as a cunning spy, and prudent negotiator. But the most celebrated part of his story consists of his adventures after the destruction of Troy, which form the subject of the Homeric poem called after him, the Odyssey. For a full account of these adventures consult *Smith's Classical Dictionary*. Returning alone to Ithaca, he was kindly received by the faithful swine-herd Eumæus, and accompanied him and Telemachus to the town where the suitors were on the following day to contend with Ulysses' bow for the prize of Penelope's hand. As none of the suitors was able to draw this bow, Ulysses took it up, began to attack the suitors, and with the aid of his son and Eumæus, slew them all except Medon. Penelope, overjoyed, recognises in the victorious stranger her long-lost Ulysses.

1. *Hanc,* sc. *epistolam.*—An ellipse frequent in English, *e. g.*, "I write this [*sc.* letter] in haste," &c., but only occurs once in the Heroides. *Epistolam* is an awkward word to get into an hexameter line. *ο εριβω (γραφω)*

Lento.—This word has not merely the force of βραδυνόστῳ: "so dilatory" in returning home, but also conveys a fond reproach that want of affection for her is the cause of his tardiness.

2. Though the meaning of this line is obvious, ("Don't answer me, but just come yourself") the true reading is a matter of great doubt. The common reading,—

"*Nil mihi rescribas ut tamen: ipse veni*"

is a solecism, for *ut tamen* ought not to be after, but before, *mihi rescribas. Attamen,* "yet however," as Cookesley justly observes, cannot be the right word. Some read, *Ah! tamen.* Bentley conjectures *tu tamen.* Distinguish *vĕni* and *vēni.*

3. *Troja jacet certe.*—"Troy, we are assured, lies low in the dust;" *that* cannot be what detains you. Observe the force of *certe.* *classis (orig. a division μεθαψο Kληγ*

Danais invisa puellis.—"Hateful to Grecian wives," on account of the long absence of their husbands at the siege of Troy. The Greeks were called *Danoi,* from Danaus, son of Belus, and brother of Ægyptus, who wandered out of Egypt into Greece, and there founded Argos. Latham thinks that the Eponymus of the Argive *Danai* was the Israelite tribe of *Dan;* an assertion which derives some weight from the fact of Dan's "dwelling in ships," and Isaiah's declaration that the sons and daughters of Judah were sold into captivity beyond the sea.

4. *Priamus*, the famous king of Troy at the time of the Trojan war, was the son of Laomedon and Strymo. His original name is said to have been Podarces "the swift-footed," which was changed into Priamus [Πρίαμος] "the ransomed" (from πρίαμαι) because he was ransomed by his sister, Hesione, after he had fallen into the hands of Hercules. His first wife was *Arisbe;* he afterwards married Hecuba by whom he had the following children: Hector, Alexander, or Paris, Deiphobus, Helenus, Polydorus, Troilus, Creüsa, Cassandra, and many others. He was killed in extreme old age, by Pyrrhus, in the storming of Troy by the Greeks.

Tanti.—" Worth so much" bloodshed and misery.

Troja.—Troy received many names from its different kings' It was called *Troja* from Tros, son of Ericthonius, and grandson of Dardanus; *Teucria* from Teucer; *Dardania* from Dardanus; *Ilium* or *Ilion* from Ilus. Troy comprised all that district to the north-west of Mysia, in Asia Minor, bounded on the west by the Ægean Sea, on the north by the Hellespont, on the east by the mountains which border on the valley of the Rhodius, and on the south by the Gulf of Adramyttium. The territory of Troy, properly called the Troad, is for the most part mountainous, being intersected by Mount Ida and its branches; the largest plain is that iu which the city of Troy stood. The chief rivers were the Satnois on the south, the Rhodius on the North, and the Simois and Scamander in the centre. These two rivers, so renowned in the legends of the Trojan war, flow from two different points in the chain of Mount Ida, and unite in the plain of Troy, through which the united stream flows northwest, and falls into the Hellespont east of the promontory of Sigeum,

5. *O utinam*, etc., cf. Hor. Odes, I. 15.

Lacedæmŏnă, acc. Gr. from *Lacedæmon,—ŏnis;* other form, *Lacedæmonem.* Sparta, the most famous city of Peloponnesus, and the capital of Menelaus, was so called from Lacedæmon, son of Jupiter and Täygete. It was while staying here as the guest of Menelaus, that Paris became enamoured of Helen.

6. *Obrutus insanis aquis,* "whelmed in the raging waves." *Esset.*—The subjunctive after *utinam.*

Adulter, "Paris."—Derived from *ad* and *alteram*.

7. *Non ego,* etc.—"I would not, in that event, have had to lie shivering," &c.

Frigida (rigeo).—Cf. φρίσσω, ῥιγέω.

8. *Relicta,* "deserted" by you.

9. *Spatiosam fallere noctem,* "to beguile the wearisome night." So *decipere noctem. Fallo* akin to Gr. σφάλλω.

10. *Viduas manus* by synecdoche for *Penelopen viduam.* *Vidua,* "widowed," is from the same root *vid,* which we have in *di-vido,* divide.

Tela, "the web," prob. contr. from *texela,* from *texo,* "I weave." The ancient looms were perpendicular, not horizontal; hence *pendula* tela.

11. *Pericula* [per, ire]. *Veris,* sc. *periculis,* "than the reality;" lit., the true dangers.

12. *Solliciti,* der. fr. obs. *Sollus* = *totus,* and *cieo.*

13. *Fingebam,* "I fancied." *In te ituros,* "would attack you."

Troas, acc. pl. Gr. from *Tros:* a Trojan.

14. "I always turned pale at the mention of the name of Hector."

15. *Antilochum.*—Antilochus was slain by the Ethiopian Memnon, son of Aurora, not by Hector. Cf. Hom. Od. IV. 187. Wherefore some scholars read *Anchialum*, others *Amphimachum*. Antilochus, son of Nestor and Eurydice, accompanied his father to Troy, and distinguished himself by his bravery. He was buried by the side of his friends Achilles and Patroclus.

Hectore.—Hector, the chief hero of the Trojans in their war with the Greeks, was the eldest son of Priam and Hecuba, the husband of Andromache, and father of Scamandrius. He fought with the bravest of the Greeks, and at length slew Patroclus, the friend of Achilles. The death of his friend roused Achilles to the fight. The other Trojans fled before him into the city. Hector alone remained without the walls, though his parents implored him to return ; but when he saw Achilles, his heart failed him and he took to flight. Thrice did he race round the city, pursued by the swift-footed Achilles, and then fell pierced by Achilles' spear. The victor tied Hector's body to his chariot, and thus dragged him into the camp of the Greeks; so Homer relates, but later traditions have it that he first dragged the body thrice around the walls of Ilium.

16. *Causa timoris,* "the object of our anxious fear."

17. *Menœtiaden.*—Patronymic term for Patroclus, son of Menœtius, and the intimate friend of Achilles. He fought bravely against the Trojans, until Achilles, after his quarrel with Agamemnon, withdrew from the scene of action, when Patroclus followed his example. But when the Greeks were hard pressed, he begged Achilles to allow him to put on his armour, and with his men to assist the Greeks. Achilles granted his request, and Patroclus, entering the lists *falsis sub armis,* "clad in armour not his own," after performing

prodigies of valour, was at length slain by Hector. To avenge his death, Achilles again took the field.

Falsis.—Adj. der. from *fallere*, "that deceived" the foe.

18. Penelope wept to think that stratagem might some time fail even the δολόμητις 'Οδυσσεύς.

19. *Tlepolemus,* a Rhodian chieftain, son of Hercules and Astyoche, was slain at Troy by Sarpedon, king of Lycia. Hence *Lycia* hasta. Lycia, a province of Asia Minor, lies on the Mediterranean Sea, between Pamphylia and Caria.

Tepefecerat [tepeo-facio.]—The construction here changes. *Si quis narrabat* is dropped and *si* only retained,-but unexpressed. Instead of "If any one had told me that Tlepolemus had, &c.," render "Had Tlepolemus [= if Tlepolemus had] warmed with his blood a Lycian spear; my anxiety, &c."

21. *Achivis* ['ΑχαιϜοί].—"Grecian," from Achaia; as also *Argolici,* v. 25, "Grecian," from Argolis. Achaia and Argolis were both prominent Peloponnesian states.

22. *Frigidius glacie.*—See note v. 7. Cf. Ovid Metam. IX. 582,—"pavet glaciali frigore pectus." Fast. I. 98.

"Et gelidum subito frigore pectus erat."

Amantis, "of your loving wife."

23. *Bene consuluit,* "benignly regarded." *Deus.* Hymenæus, aut aliquis alius. *Amori,* dat. commodi.

24. *In cinerem.*—Loers reads *in cineres;* but VII. MSS. have *cinerem.* See also Ovid, Metam. II. 216, "In cinerem vertunt."

Sospite viro, "and my husband safe." Abl. absolute.

Sospes, akin to σῶς. Vir. = ἀνήρ.

25. *Argolici* = Argivi ['ΑργειϜοί.]—See note, v. 21. *Rediere duces,* i.e., Agamemnon, Menelaus, and Nestor. Their re-

turn makes Penelope all the more solicitous about the fate
of her husband, who, though Troy had fallen years ago, had
not yet returned to Ithaca.

Altaria fumant, " the altars smoke," *i.e.*, with incense and
victims. *Altaria* [fr. *altus*] primarily meant that which is
placed *high* upon the altar (*ara*) for the burning of the victim.
Hence, poet. (as *pars pro toto*) *a high altar*, built and orna-
mented with more splendour than the *ara*.

26. *Barbara*, " foreign," *i.e.*, Trojan. The Greeks called all
nations without the Hellenic pale βάρβαροι. The name is
probably derived from the Berbers, a tribe of Africa: the
people of modern Barbary. Some assert the word to be of
Phœnician or Jewish origin—Bar, " son of," (as, Bar-Jonas,
Bar-Timæus), frequently entering into their nomenclature,
like the Scottish *Mac*, German *Fitz;* so that the Greeks called
them all βάρβαροι.

Præda [akin to *præs*, Eng. *prize*] " spoil." Arms and spoil
taken from the enemy were consecrated to the Gods, and
hung up in the temples.

27. *Nymphæ* [Νύμφαι] = *nuptæ*, " wives." *Nympha* means
either an inferior goddess, *a nymph;* or *a married*—never an
unmarried—*woman. Nymphæ* here, doubtless, means the wives
of Grecian notables.

Dona = ἀναθήματα, " offerings to the gods."

28. *Illi* (i.e., mariti ipsi) *canunt*. Their husbands relate in
glowing terms how the fates of Troy were overcome by their
own. Cookesley badly connects *canunt* with *hymns of thanks-
giving*. These would be left to the Rhapsodists by the scarred
veterans of the Trojan campaign. *Canunt* here is elegantly
used for *narrant.* Cf. v. 30.

Fata, pl. of *fatum*, fr. *fari*, " the divine decrees." These

fata of the Trojans, retaining which they could not be con-
quered, were—1. The life of Troilus, son of Priam; Achilles
slew him. 2. The conservation of the Palladium, or image
of Pallas; Ulysses and Diomede entered the city by night,
and, having slain the garrison of the citadel, carried it off.
3. The horses of Rhesus, if they were not taken before that

"Pabula gustassent Trojæ Xanthumque bibissent."—*Virg*.

They were stolen by Ulysses and Diomede. 4. The tomb of
Laomedon, at the Scæan gate; this was violated by the Trojans themselves when they pulled down the gate to admit the
wooden horse. Thus were the *Troica fata* overcome *suis*
(fatis). Cf. Virg. Æn. VII. 293,—

——— "fatis contraria nostris
Fata Phrygum."

29. *Mirantur* governs *ea* [quæ referuntur] understood.
Justi senes in contradistinction to *trepidæ puellæ;* "dis-
criminating old men," who therefore only admire those things
which appear to be true and worthy admiration, and "timid
maidens," whose credulous, unsophisticated natures lead them
to admire everything.

30. *Conjux*, from *con* and *jugum:* the idea of *yoking* or
coupling. Compare Gr. σύζυγος [σὺν and ζυγόν] and δάμαρ
[δαμᾶν = *domare*, to tame], and St. Paul: "Be ye not un-
equally *yoked together* with unbelievers."

Pendet ab ore, "hangs upon the lips." So Virgil says of
Dido, Æn. IV. 79:

——— "pendetque iterum narrantis ab ore."

31. *Aliquis*, "many a one." *Posita*, "placed before him."
Monstrat, "describes."

The Greeks after supper poured out some unmixed wine on

the table as a libation to the " good spirit" (ἀγαθοῦ δαίμονος).
To this custom Penelope here alludes. So Tibul. I. Eleg. XI.
31 :

> " Ut mihi potanti possit sua dicere facta,
> Miles, et *in mensa pingere castra mero.*"

32. *Pingit,* etc., " And maps out all Troy in a few wine-
drops."

Pergămŭ,—*ōrum* [Πέργαμα: akin to πύργος, a tower]. *The
citadel of Troy,* poet. for *Troy* itself.

Mero, "unmixed wine;" *vinum,* wine in general.

33. *Simois,*—*entis,* a small river of Troas, which falls into
the Scamander, now *Mendes.* See note, v. 4.

Sīgēiă, poet. for *Trojana.* Sigēum was a promontory in
Troas, where Achilles was buried, now *Cape Janissary.*

34. *Priami senïs.*—Homer, and after him, Virgil, represent
Priam as old and full of years. *Celsa,* a part. fr. an obs.
verb *cello* [Th. κέλλω]. ι ἡραιων (ἵ π π ο ς)

35. *Æacides,* " Achilles," the grandson of Æacus.

Tendebat, [Th. τείνω,] "spread his tent." Cf. Virg. XI. 29 :

> " Hic Dolopum manus, hic sævus *tendebat* Achilles."

(ςω) 36. *Lacer Hector,* " The mangled (corpse of) Hector." Homer
(Il. XXII. 369–371) says that after Achilles killed Hector, the
Greeks crowded round to gaze on the dead body of the distinguished warrior, and that no one beheld it without inflicting
a wound. No wonder that his bleeding corpse, so lacerated,
terrified the horses (*admissos*) " as they ran at full speed."

37. *Misso.*—This is a piece of dissimulation on Penelope's
part. She did not send Telemachus. He went at Minerva's
suggestion, without his mother's knowledge. Homer, Od. II.
Quærere, by an elegant Græcism for *ut quæreret.*

38. *Nestor,* here called *Senior.* Homer represents him as

having lived three generations. So Horace, Odes, II. 9, 14, calls him " ter ævo functus senex," and Attius, " Trisæcli-senex." He was king of Pylos, and father of Antilochus, renowned for his wisdom, his eloquence, his justice, and his knowledge of war.

39. *Rhesum.*—Rhesus, the son of Eïoneus, king of Thrace. He came to the assistance of Troy with his steeds, white as the snow and fleet as the wind. If these should once drink the waters of the Xanthus, and feed upon the grass of the Trojan plain, an oracle had declared that Troy should never fall. But as soon as Rhesus had reached the Trojan territory, and, wearied with the march, had pitched his camp (*Thracia castra,* v. 42), late at night, Ulysses and Diomede, informed of these facts by Dolon, a Trojan spy, whom they had intercepted in a night adventure, penetrated into his camp, slew Rhesus himself (*proditum somno*) "betrayed by sleep," and carried off his horses.

Dolona [Δόλωνα] acc. Gr. of *Dolon,—onis.* He was slain by Diomede.

40. *Hic,* i.e., Rhesus, used here for *alter; Hic* usually refers to the nearest.

Dolo, a very disagreeable homœoteleuton with the following pentameter. Bentley reads *metu;* others, *vigil* and *loco.* It appears to be a petty paronomasia on Dolon's name, or else an oversight of Ovid. Impunity was promised Dolon by Ulysses and Diomede if he would reveal what was passing in the Trojan camp. Having received the required information about Rhesus and his horses, they treacherously slew him: a contemptible *dolus,* scarcely justified by the sentiment, " All's fair in war."

41. *Tuorum,* i.e., of me and Telemachus; gov. by *oblite. Recordor, memini, obliviscor,* &c., gov. the genitive.

c

42. *Thracia castra.* See note v. 39. *Tangere,* " to attack.'』 Another reading is *frangere,* " to break up "

43. *Tot viros.*—Rhesus and his twelve comrades. *Uno,* i.e., Diomede.

44. *At bene,* etc.—Affectionate irony. *Ante = antea,* adv.

45. *Usque metu micuere sinus.*—" My bosom kept trembling with constant fear." *Micuere,* fr. *micare.* "Swift motion," and its usual consequences in the sun's rays, "glittering light," are sometimes convertible terms in Latin and Greek. Compare ἀργός, αἰόλος.

Dum = donec. Amicum per agmen, "through the friendly lines " [of the Greeks].

46. *Dictus es,* i.e., *a Telemacho.* Penelope is repeating here from *Ausus es,* v. 41, to *equis,* v. 46, a thrilling episode of the story told her by Telemachus on his return from his visit to the Pylian Nestor.

Ismariis = Thraciis.—Ismarus was a mountain and city of Thrace, celebrated for its wines.

47. *Mihi,* dat. com after *prodest. Vestris lacertis,* " by the strong arms of you Greeks." *Lacertus* is the muscular part of the arm, from the elbow to the shoulder ; *brachium,* the arm from the elbow to the hand. *Vester* is never used for *tuus.* Bentley reads *Graiis* for *vestris.*

48. *Ῑl̆ŏs,* fem. " Troy." So called from Ilus, son of Tros. Another form is *Ilium,* or *Ilion,* neut.

Solum, [Eng. *soil*] " level ground," nom. to *prodest.*

49. *Troja durante,* abl. abs. " While Troy was holding out."

50. *Dempto fine carendus,* " to be regretted " (*i.e.,* to be absent) "for ever ;" literally, "all end being taken away.'

57. *Aliis,* "for others," dat. com. *Uni mihi—restant,* "survives for me alone." Penelope means that, whereas her husband had not returned to her, although Troy had been

destroyed, it might as well have been standing as far as she was concerned.

52. *Incola victor.*—A line of vigorous poetry : " which the victorious colonist ploughs with his captive steer." *Incola*, Th. *in* and *colo*. *Captivo* [capio] *i.e.*, taken from the Trojans.

53. *Seges*, " corn-land."

54. *Luxuriat*, " produces abundant crops."
Phrygio, " Trojan." Troy was situated in Phrygia Minor.
Pinguis, [πίων, fat.] " rendered fruitful."

55. *Aratris*, fr. *aratrum*, Gr. ἄροτρον.

56. *Herba*, [akin to φέρβω, to pasture] " the grass."

57. *Victor*, Th. *vin-co*, Eng. *win*. *Quæ* (sit tibi) *causa*.

58. *Quo—orbe*, "in what part of the world, iron-hearted one, you may be lurking." *Lateas.*—Jealousy lurks in this word.

59. *Peregrinam*, " foreign," fr. *per* and *agros*. *Hæc littora*, i.e., of Ithaca. *Puppim* [Eng. *poop*.] " the stern ;" because sailors in ancient times on coming into port turned the stern toward the shore. Cf. Virgil, " stant littore puppes."

60. *Mihi* = *a me*. *Multa rogatus*, " After having been asked many questions."

61. *Tibi reddat*, " may hand to thee." Distinguish *usquam* and *unquam*.

62. *Digitis charta notata meis*, " a letter written with my own hands." This is a poetic anachronism. It is scarcely probable that writing materials were known at the assigned date of the Trojan war, B.C. 1184.

63. *Pylon*, acc. Gr. of *Pylos*. There were three cities of this name in Peloponessus ; in Elis, in Messenia, and in Triphylia. The latter was the Pylos founded by Neleus, and governed by his son Nestor ; hence called " *Nēlēă arva*."

64. *Misimus.*—Consult note, v. 37. *Incerta fama*, "no certain tidings."

65. *Sparten*, Gr. acc. here elegantly put for *Menelaum*, king of Argos, whom Telemachus also visited, but could get no satisfactory intelligence of his father. See note post. v. 98.

66. *Lentus.*—See note v. 1.

67. *Mœnia Phœbi.*—Poetic pleonasm for *Troja.* Apollo and Neptune having displeased Jove, were doomed to serve Laomedon, king of Troy, for wages. They accordingly built the walls of Troy. Laomedon refusing to pay the stipulated hire, Neptune sent a sea-monster to whom, from time to time, a maiden, chosen by lot, had to be sacrificed. On one occasion, the lot falling on Hesione, daughter of Laomedon, Hercules promised to rescue her if Laomedon would give him the horses which Tros had received from Jove, as a compensation for Ganymedes. Laomedon promised, but again broke his word when Hercules had killed the monster and saved Hesione. Hercules, thereupon, slew Laomedon with all his sons, except Podarces (Priam), whom Hesione ransomed with her veil, hence called Priamus (fr. πρίαμαι). Apollo, in Ov. Heroid. v. 135, is also called " *Trojæ Munitor.*"

68. *Votis meis*, dat. " with my wishes." *Levis*, " thoughtless."

69. *Tantum*, adv. " only." Jealousy again.

70. *Cum multis* [*querelis*] = *cum multarum querelis.* Penelope complains that she is

" Denied, though sought with tears, the sad relief
Which misery loves, the fellowship of grief."

71. *Quid timeam*, " what I am to fear." *Ignoro*, from *in*, neg., and *gnoro* [gnarus] "I know." The old form *gn* is represented in English by *kn;* as, *gnod-us*, a *knot*, *gnav-us*, a *knave*. *Demens* [de, mens] " in my madness."

72. " And a wide field is open for my anxieties."

73. *Suspicor*, fr. *sub* and *spicere*, " to look up from below;" hence, to suspect. Cf. Gr. ὑπόδρα, fr. ὑπὸ and δέρκομαι.

75. *Quæ vestra libido est,* " such is the capriciousness of you men." *Vester.* See note on v. 47.

76. *Potes esse captus,* " you may be ensnared."

77. *Quam rustica sit tibi conjux,* " How countrified a wife you've got." ℓ cα∧α (Λ ℳ Ѵ ο ѕ)

78. " Who only does not allow wool to be unused," *i.e.* " only knows enough to spin."

79. *Fallar.*—Supply *utinam.* " That I may be in error, and that this suspicion," &c. *Crimen,* lit. a charge [κρίνω.]

80. " And may you not choose to be absent, though you have the power to return ! " *i.e.,* I trust your absence is not caused by your own will.

81. *Viduo discedere lecto,* i.e., to marry some one else.

82. *Cogit* [*co-ago*] " urges." *Immensas,* Th. *in* and *metior.*

83. *Increpet usque.* " constantly inveighs against."

85. *Pietate,* &c., " by my dutiful affection and chaste entreaties." *Pudicis,* i.e , *pudicæ uxoris.*

86. *Frangitur = flectitur. Vires temperat,* " does not exercise to the full his paternal authority."

87. A line evidently taken from Homer's Odyssey, IX. 24 :

Δουλίχιόν τε Σάμη τε καὶ ὑλήεσσα Ζάκυνθος.

Same (now *Cephallenia*), *Zacynthos* (now *Zante*), are islands in the Ionian sea, near Ithaca (now *Teaki*). *Dulichium* is also named by other poets besides Homer, as an island in the same sea; but it is not known what island is meant. It is supposed to have been one of the group called the Echinades.

Tulit = protulit.

88. *Turba luxuriosa,* " a wanton crowd," in apposition to *proci,* " suitors." Penelope might well style them " a wanton crowd," " an unruly crew," for, according to Hom. Od XVI. 247, she had fifty-two suitors from Dulichium, twenty-four from Samos, twenty from Zacynthos, and twelve from Ithaca.

They acted very imperiously and wasted Ulysses' substance in riotous living. *Proci* [Gr. μνηστῆρες] from an old verb *procure* (akin to *precari*) = *poscere in matrimonium*

89. This and the following line are highly calculated to incense Ulysses and bring him home.

90. *Viscera*, "means of living," in apposition to *opes*, "property." *[handwritten]*

Nostra, i.e., of Laertes, Telemachus and me.

Dilaniantur.—Another reading is *dilacerantur.*

91. Penelope now gives a list of the suitors who courted and plundered her in a chivalrous, off-hand kind of a way, at one and the same time; but, strange to say, Ovid not only places *Medon* among the number, but adds the epithet *dirum*, whereas Homer represents him as an excellent person and (Od. XXII. 357), a great friend of Telemachus, on which account he was spared by his father Ulysses, when the rest of the suitors were slain. Bentley tries to get over the difficulty by reading *dium*, which badly suits the context. This makes the third remarkable discrepancy between Homer and Ovid which I have noticed in this Epistle. The other two are in vv. 15 and 37. *[handwritten]*

92. Icarius, Penelope's father, wished her to marry Eurymachus. *Avidas Antinoique manus.* Poetic pleonasm for *Avidumque Antinoum.*

93. *Turpiter—alis*, "you nourish to your disgrace;" better than *turpiter absens*, "basely absent." *[handwritten]*

94. *Rebus—partis*, "wealth purchased." Distingush *partīs* and *partĭs. Sanguine.*—Wealth, in the Heroic Age, was considered at least as honorably acquired by predatory warfare, as by tilling the ground or by herding the flock.

95. *Irus*, an insolent beggar in the house of Ulysses, at Ithaca.. *[handwritten]*

Melanthius was the goat-herd of Ulysses, by whom he was put to death for his dishonesty, insolence, and treachery.

Pecoris, fr. *pecus*, "sheep," whence *pecunia*, money, the product of the sale of wool. *Actor, ab agendo*, Th. *agere*. *Edendi*, "to be eaten," by the suitors, from *ed-o*, Eng. *eat; d* and *t* being interchangeable.

96. *Ultimus pudor*, (*nominativus pendens*) "a crowning disgrace," when even a beggar and a goat-herd dare insolently squander your property.

97. *Tres—imbelles*, ["only] three, and ill fitted to contend with them ;" (*in* neg. and *bellum*).

98. *Laertes*, king of Ithaca, son of Acrisius and Chalcomedusa, and father of Ulysses by Anticlea. Some writers call Ulysses the son of Sisyphus. Laertes was still alive when his long-lost son returned to Ithaca.

Senex.—So Hom. Od. XXIV. 233, γήραϊ τειρόμενος.

Telemachus, son of Ulysses and Penelope. He was still an infant when his father went to Troy ; and when the latter had been absent from home nearly twenty years, Telemachus went to Pylos and Sparta to gather information respecting him. He was hospitably received by the Pylian Nestor, as also by Menelaus, at Sparta, who told him the prophecy of Proteus concerning Ulysses. To excite Ulysses' pity, Penelope calls Telemachus, already in his twentieth year, *puer*. Similarly, v. 115, she styles herself *puellam*.

99. *Insidias* (in, sedeo). The suitors lay in wait for Telemachus, hoping to intercept him on his return home from Pylos. *Nuper*, [*noviper* fr. *novus*] "not long ago."

100. *Invitis omnibus.*—This seems irreconcilable with the statement in v. 63, that Penelope sent Telemachus. Bentley conjectures *ignaris*, which leaves the difficulty nearly as great as before, but which corresponds more closely with the

Homeric version of the story. See note v. 37. All were ignorant except the old nurse, Euryclea.

101. *Ordine,* "in their natural order." She prays that the Fates may take the oldest first.

102. *Comprimat,* [*con, premo*] "may close in death." The closing the eyes of the deceased by the hands of friends appears to have been a very ancient custom. Homer mentions it in Od. XI. 426, and Euripides in the Hecuba.

103. *Hoc faciunt,* i e., *precantur,* "have the same wish—offer the same prayer." *Facere* often usurps the sense of the leading verb, which precedes it.   *munnun dus*
                                                                              (ĩn̄ ru
Custos boum, Philætius. *Nutrix,* Euryclēa.

104. *Tertius, i.e.,* Eumæus, the faithful swineherd, who assisted Ulysses and Telemachus in slaying the suitors. *Cura fidelis.*—Metonymy for *qui fideliter curat.* *ev λu (gualo)*

105. *Ut qui sit,* "inasmuch as he is." *Armis.*—Another reading is *annis,* "by reason of his age;" but the expression *inutilis armis* is very frequent in Ovid. Cf. Fasti, II. 238, III. 173, V. 81. And besides, the mention of *hostibus* would point to *armis* as the true reading.

106. *Hostibus,* i.e., *procis.*

107. *Vivat modo.*—Understand *si.*

108. *Illa,* sc. *ætas,* "For the present that (tender age) ought to be protected by the aid of his father." *Auxilium,* when used in the plural number, *generally* signifies "auxiliary troops."

109. *Inimicos,* personal enemies of Penelope's; *hostes,* as to Laertes, v. 106. Distinguish *inimicus* and *hostis.* By the nice use of these expressions, Penelope seeks to commend her faithful love to Ulysses. *Pellere = ad pellendos.*

110 *Ara,* "an altar of refuge." *Portus et aura* is an elegant reading, both tropes being taken from Ulysses' sea-faring

life : a safe port and a favouring breeze—the two delights of a mariner.

111. *Mollibus annis*, " tender years ;" when the mind is easily *moulded*. *Mollis*, qu. *movilis*, fr. *moveo*.   *annus* (ἐνο

112. *Erudiendus* [*e* and *rudis*] " Ought to have been in-ᵃ ᵃ,ᵘ structed in his father's arts," as a warrior and king.

113. *Respice* [*re* and obs. *spicere.*]—Ineffable *pity* shines in this word. *Condas*, [*con, do*] " may close." See v. 102.

114. *Sustinet*, [*sub, teneo*] "He bears up under the evils which fate allots to extreme old age."   *ars* (ἀρ ω)

115. *Te discedente*, " when you left " for Troy. *Puella.*— See note, v. 98.   *annus - ως*

116. *Protinus* [*pro, tenus.*]—*Ut* = *quamvis* "even though."

Considerable poetic art is manifested in the structure of the closing lines of this beautiful epistle. Commencing at v. 97, we have a distich containing the *tres imbelles :* three points of attraction which are to lure the truant Ulysses to his sea-girt home : his loving wife, his aged sire, his promising son. Holding up her boy, the pledge of their early love, in the next six lines, (vv. 99-104) Penelope makes a touching appeal to a father's heart by an allusion to the dangers which beset him, and the filial offices he should perform for them in the closing scenes of life. "Laertes, Telemachus, and I," occupy the next six lines, a distich to each (the true notion of Elegiac poetry) again with delicate touches pourtraying the urgent necessity for a speedy return. And again, in the three concluding distiches, the boy of tender years who should be receiving a father's instruction, the aged father, only waiting his son's return that he may close his eyes in death, and the wife, left in the bloom of youth, fearful lest her personal charms should have suffered by the long absence of her lord, all present a picture, as charming as it is natural, as full of home affection and conjugal love, as ever won back the admiration and esteem of vagrant mariner.

EPIST. XIII.

Laodamia (Λαοδάμεια).—Daughter of Acastus, and wife of Protesilaus. When her husband was slain before Troy, she begged the gods to be allowed to converse with him for only three hours. The request was granted. Hermes led Protesilaus back to the upper world, and when Protesilaus died a second time, Laodamia died with him. A later tradition states that Laodamia made an image of her husband, to which she paid divine honors : but as her father Acastus interfered, and commanded her to burn the image, she herself leaped into the fire and expired.

Protesilao (Πρωτεσιλάῳ).—Protesilaus was the son of Iphiclus and Astyoche. His native place was Phylace, in Thessaly; hence he is called Phylacides. He sailed for Troy with forty ships, according to Homer, snd brought with him many Thessalian warriors. He was the first of all the Greeks who was killed by the Trojans, being the first who landed on the Trojan shore. According to the common tradition, he was slain by Hector. Protesilaus is most celebrated in ancient story for the strong affection existing between him and his wife Laodamia. His tomb was shewn near Eleus, in the Thracian Chersonese, where a magnificent temple was erected to him.

1. *Mittit*, fr. *mitto*, "I make to go," "I send," causative form of *meo*, I go. The order of these first two involved lines is : *Laodamia, amans Æmonis, mittit salutem viro Æmo-*

nio et optat ire, quo mittitur [*salus*]. Another interpretation makes *ire* = *pervenire*, and understands *salutem* before it; i.e., *wishes the letter (salutem) to arrive* at the place *whither it is sent* Not so good.

Optat [Gr. ὔπτω] governs *ire*.

Salutem [fr. *sulvus*].—*Salus*, a wish for one's welfare, ex*pressed vivâ voce or in writing; here, in writing, and hence *salutem* (*pars pro toto*) here = *epistolam*.

2. *Æmŏnĭs,-ĭdis*, adj. fem. = *Thessala*. Thessaly was called Æmonia, from Æmonia, one of the daughters of Deucalion, who gave her name to that district.

3. *Aulide.*—*At* a place of the third declension is put in the ablative. Aulis, a sea-port town of Bœotia, where the Greeks were detained by stress of weather, through the anger of Diana on account of a stag slain by the unconscious Agamemnon, who had to immolate his daughter Iphigenia to appease the offended deity. ~~nvi (ahm nvi + is.~~

Est fama, [fr. *fari*, as φάμα fr. φήμι] "There is a rumour."

4. *Hic—ventus*, "Where was this wind?" *i.e.* which would have detained you at home with me. *Ventus* appears to be derived from the common root of *venio*, and *veho*, signifying "motion along with, or towards." *Fugeres*, said reproachfully; non enim *fugit* Protesilaus.

5. *Freta* [Eng. *Frith.*]—*Fretum* originally meant a *sound* or *channel*; afterwards used for *the sea*.

Distinguish *frĕta* and *frēta*.

Vestris remis, "the oars of your crew." See note, Ep. 1, 47.

Remis, [Gr. ἐρέτμος] dative after *obsistere*.

6. *Sævis.*—*Sævus* means "roused to fierceness;" *ferus*, "naturally fierce." "That time was suitable for stormy billows." *Utile*, because it would have kept you here at home.

7. *Mandata*, [*in manus do*, I give in charge] "injunctions, *i.e.*, to take care of yourself, &c.

9. *Raptus* [Gr. ἁρπάζω.] *Hinc*, i.e., from Phylace, in Thessaly.

Præceps [*præ-caput*, *head-foremost*] "in precipitate haste." *Tua vela vocaret*, " invited your sails," *i.e.*, persuaded you to set off.

10. *Nautæ*, contracted form of *navitæ*, [navis, ναῦς] dat. *com.*

11. *Aptus*, from an obsolete verb, *apo*, [Gr. ἅπτω, to fit] "suited to," "favorable for."

12. *Amplexus*, "embrace," fr. *amplector*, am = ἀμφι (circum) plecti = πλέκεσθαι, *to twine round* a person.

13. *Verba*, digammated from root ἔρω, εἴρω, to speak. *Imperfecta*, [*in*, neg. *per*, *facio*.] *Reliquit* is preferred by some because *potui* follows, and some, also, read *potuit* sc. *lingua*.

14. *Vale* [Eng. *well*] is a noun here.

15. *Incubuit* "pressed upon," *i.e.*, blew violently. *Boreas* [Βορέας] would be the favorable wind to convey him from Thessaly to Aulis. *Abrepta* [*ab rapio*.]

Vela, contracted from *vehulum*, from *veho*, like *eo*, *venio*, *ventus*, conveying idea of motion. *Tetendit* [τείνω.] This is a very vigorous line, and to one accustomed to boating would seem a beautiful example of onomatopœia, the sound according finely with the sense.

16. *Jam*, [*déjà*, old Fr. *ja*.] " Already," denotes the swiftness of the action.

17. *Juvabat*, gov. *me* understood.

19. *Ut—non poteram*. *Ut* has force of *quum*. "When I was no longer able."

20. *Vultus meos*, "my longing gaze." *Vultus*, the countenance as to *features* and *expression*, frequently meaning " angry looks ;" *facies*, the *face*.

mens (~~*vultus*~~ strength)

21. *Fugacia* [Homer, φυζακινά].

22. *Pontus*, [Gr. πόντος, Eng. *pond*] "the open sea."

23. *Tenebris obortis*, abl. abs. *Tenebræ*, "the darkness or dimness of a swoon." *Obortis*, fr. *oborior* [Gr. ὄρνυμι, ὄρω, Eng. *arise*.] *Castus (candeo*

24· *Succiduo* [*sub*, from under, *cado*.] *Dicor*, because in swooning, her senses left her; she can therefore only speak from what her friends told her. *Genu*, Gr. γόνυ, fr. common root *gen* or *gne*; Eng. *knee*. See note, Ep. 1, 71. *Qcer (εῖκνρ*

25. *Iphiclus*, son of Phylacus, and father of Protesilaus. *Grandævus* [*grande-ævum*.] *Acastus*, father of Laodamia.

26. *Refecit*, "restored me." *ficeto ire pexui pexi*

27. *Pium*, not *pious*, but *affectionate. fuctiwi pexum +*

28. *Miseræ*, dat. after *licuisse. fu ettum (πεκτεω*

29. *Pariter*, "as well."

31. *Pectendos*, "to be arranged," by my tire-woman.

32. *Capillos*, [*caput*] "tresses."

32. *Aurata*, [*aurum*, Fr. *or*, Ital. *oro*] "inwoven with gold."

33. *Ut quas*, "*Like* [the Bacchantes] *whom*."

Pampinea—hasta, "the thyrsus," or magic wand of Bacchus, generally a spear-staff, round which vine-leaves were entwined. *Bicorniger*, [*bis*, *cornua*, *gero*] "the two-horned god." Bacchus was frequently represented with horns. Cookesley thinks Bacchus was so called because the *horn* was the emblem of power, Bacchus being fabled to be a great Oriental conqueror. I think Bacchus receives this epithet because wine infuses strength and vigour. Cf. Hor. Odes, III. 21, 18, "*addit cornua pauperi*." *nimius (ire mis ahin meta metion)*

34. *Furor*, "phrensy."

35. *Phylăcĕīdĕs*, Gr. nom. pl. of *Phylaceis-idis*, fem. "Thessalian." *Phylăcē*, [Φυλακή,] a city of Thessaly where Prote-

silaus reigned; hence he is called *Phylacides.* Some read *Phyllēides.*

36. *Indue.* [Gr. ἔνδυε.] Hence Eng. *endue.*

Laodamia, from λάος, δαμάω, like Protesilaus, from πρῶτος, λάος, both indicate an aristocratic or regnant class. Hyginus says Protesilaus was so called because he was the first of all the people to land. *Sinus,* i.e., *vestem.*

37. *Scilicet,* "I suppose, forsooth!" *Murice,* "purple;" properly, a shell-fish, from which a purple dye was extracted. *Gerere vestes,* "to wear clothes" *Gerere bella,* "to wage war."

38. *Bella geret,* antithetic̊ to *geram vestes. Iliacis,* "Trojan." Distinguish *moenia* and *murus.*

39. *Comas pectar.* An elegant græcism. Some, however, read *pectam Galea,* "helmet," usually of leather, whereas the *cassis* is of metal-plate; neither of them a very comfortable head-piece. *αͺνͺμͺ (αρͺω)*

40. *Novas vestes,* opposed to *dura arma,* and governed by *ferat.* The balance of antitheses in this and the preceding lines is very fine. *Vir,* as *ille,* in v. 39, refers to the man κατ᾽ ἐξόχην : Protesilaus.

41. *Qua possum,* "as far as I can." *Qua,* sc. *via.* Others have *quo,* sc. *squalore. Squalor,* "neglect of personal appearance." (*αͺͺυͺαͺͺ σκελλω*)

42. *Tristis agam,* "I will pass in mourning."

43. *Dyspari Priamide,* "Ill-fated Paris, Priam's evil son!" Both Greek vocatives fr. *Dysparis, idos.* [cf Hom. Il. III. 39, Δύσπαρι, εἶδος ἄριστε] and *Priamides, æ,* Gr. patronymic, from Πριαμίδης-ου. The common reading, *Dux Pari Priamide,* seems very clumsy. The Greek Δύς in composition has the force of *malum* as well as *infelix.* Therefore, in my translation, I

have, by an easy turn, added the implied *malum* to *Priamide*. *Damno*, dat. *incommodi*. *Formose* = εἶδος ἄριστε, Hom.

44. *Hos-tis, hos-pes.*—A somewhat frigid paronomasia. *Hospes* is akin to *hostis*, primarily a stranger, = a stranger who is treated as a guest.

Iners, " cowardly."—*Malus* means " cowardly" as well as " evil." Paris was the guest of Menelaus just before he eloped with Helen.

45. *Tænariæ—maritæ*, "Helen, your Grecian wife." *Tænărum* (now.*Cape Matapan*), a promontory of Laconia, and the southernmost point of Peloponessus. *Tænariæ*, adj. poet. for *Græcæ*. *Faciem*, see note, v. 20. ·

Culpasse, contr. for *culpavisse*, "had found fault with." Laodamia thus reasons : If Paris had not admired Helen, he would not have loved her, would not have carried her off ; if she had not been captivated by his personal attractions (*formosus*, v. 43), she would not have eloped with him ; there would have been no war, and my husband would have been at home with me.

46. *Tuam*, sc. *faciem*.

47. *Pro rapto*, " to recover your runaway wife."

Nimium, "excessively—much more than she is worth."

48. *Multis flebilis*, cf. Hor. Od. I. 24, 9. Take *quam* with *eris*, not with *multis*

49. *Sinistrum*, " inauspicious." Laodamia deprecates the wrath of the gods for having said *multis flebilis*, and hopes her fears may prove unfounded. The use of "omen *sinistrum*" here is very appropriate, coming from a Greek ; for, in auspices and divinations, the Romans turned the face towards the south, and so had the eastern, or fortunate, side on their left ; while the Greeks, turning to the north, had it on their right.

NOTES.

48   NOTES.

50. *Det*, "offer up." *Reduci—Jovi*, "To Jupiter who restored him in safety." It was customary for returning warriors to hang up their armour in the temples, and offer sacrifices for their safe return. Distinguish *redŭci* [redux] and *redūci*.

51. *Subit* == *in mentem venit*, "comes into my mind."

52. *More*, abl. of *manner*. *De more* is frequently used. *Nivis.* —You will notice little difference in sound between *nivis*, gen. of *nix*, and *νίφος*, gen. of *νίψ*. *Lacrymæ*, akin to Gr. *δάκρυα*. *madeo ere -ui (μα δ'άκω)*

53. *Ilion—Simoisque.*—See note, Ep. I. v. 4.   ·

Tenedos, an island off the coast of Troy. *Xanthus*, a river, and *Ide* a mountain of Troy.

55. *Nec rapere ausurus—hospes erat*, "nor was the stranger (Paris), likely to dare to run off," with Helen.

56. *Noverat*, fr. nosco ; old form, *gnosco*, Eng. *know*. Consult note, Ep. I. 71.

57. *Spectabilis*, "an object of wonderment" to the frugal Spartan people. *Auro*, abl. of *cause*.

58. "A prince who carried about on his person the wealth of Phrygia."

59. *Classe virisque*, "army and navy." *Potens*, supply *venerat*. *Per quæ*, some read *per quos*, referring to *viris*. For the rules regulating the gender and number of adjectives which refer to several substantives, see your Lat. Gram.

60. "And (yet only) a very small part of (the military force of) his kingdom accompanies him." *Quotacunque pars*, i.e., *quam exigua pars*. Another reading is *quota quemque*.

61. *His*, i.e., by Paris's brilliant display and well-appointed retinue. *Victam* (*esse*). *Consors—gemellis*, "sister to the twins," Castor and Pollux.

Ledæa, "daughter of Leda." *gemellus (gemini*

62. *Suspicor.*—See note, Ep. I. 74. *Danais*, dat. *incom.*—See note, Ep. I. 3.

Danais nocere, " to work the Greeks woe."

63. *Hectora—nescio quem,* "one Hector;" lit. "Hector, I now not who he may be." Paris had been boasting in Greece f Hector's martial prowess. This was all Laodamia knew bout him, but she had fearful misgivings of some mishap efalling her husband by Hector's hands. Her worst fears .rere realized, for, as we have seen above, Protesilaus fell by he bloody hand (*sanguinea manu*) of Hector. *Hectora,* like *Iectŏrăs,* v. 68, Gr. acc. sing. and plural of Hector ['Ἐκτώρ.] ee note, Ep. I. 15.

64. *Ferrea,* " cruel."

65. *Quisquis is est, si sum.* Note the sigmatismus. Euri-ides is charged with being fond of concurrences of the letter (sigma).

67. *Vitaris,* contr. for *vitaveris.*

69. *Facito* [ut] *dicas,* "see that you say." Some read *ut* s it does not affect the scansion.

Pugnare, [Gr. πύξ, Eng. "box."]

70. *Parcere sibi.* Laodamia intimates that if her husband erishes she will also die.

71. *Si fas est,* " If it is heaven's decree." *Fas,* "divine law," s opposed to *jus,* "human law." *Argolico—milite,* " Grecian oldiery." See note, Ep. I. 25.

72. *Non ullum* = *nullum. Vulnus,* old form, *volnus. (culeus-ec ολλυμι*

73. *Pugnet,* etc. A similar sentiment to that of Jeannette n the French ballad, " *To Jeannot :*"

> " All the world should be at peace,
>   And if kings must show their might,
>   Then let those who have the quarrels be,
>   The only men who fight."

D

74. The construction is : *Ut rapiat Paridi (eam), quam Paris ante (rapuit) sibi.* Verbs of *taking away* govern accusative and dative.

75. *Irruat* [*in, ruo*] supposes here, *exposure to danger :* "Let him rush on to the attack ;" don't you be venturesome.

Causā, etc., " And let him also conquer in the field of arms (him) whom he overcomes in the justness of his cause."

76. *Mediis,* Gr. μέσος, Eng. *midst.*

77. *Dispar,* " unlike " that of Menelaus, not Paris, as Cookesley has it ; for you have a wife at home, therefore do you only fight to live and return to the affectionate embrace of your faithful Laodamia.   *pareo (pareus ahun Παρ̄pos)*

79. *Dardanidæ.*—See note Ep. I. 4.   By a felicitous turn of the diction, Laodamia apostrophizes the Trojans as if present.

80. *Meus—sanguis,* " my life-blood ;" because she was so wrapt up in him, that the continuation of her own life depended on his.   I think this line plainly indicates the true reading of the last line of this Epistle to be *" si tibi cura mei,"* not *" sit tibi cura mei."*

81. *Fateor,* [fr. Gr. φάω, φήμι] " now I confess," what before I dared not say for fear of using ill-omened speech.

Volui, [akin to βούλομαι] "I wished to call you back, and my mind was leading me " to recall you.   Distinguish *animus, anima,* and *mens.*

82. *Substitit,* " stood still."   *Auspicii,* derived from *avis— spicere,* here simply means "omen ;" lit., *augury from birds.*

83. *Foribus,* fr. foris, Gr. θύρα, Eng. *door.*

84. *Pes, pedis,* Gr. πούς, πόδος, " Your foot gave an ill omen by stumbling on the threshold," which among the ancients was considered unlucky.   *Offenso limine,* abl. abs. ; lit., " the threshold having been struck by it."

86. Poor Laodamia tries to avert the consequence of this mishap by prayer.

87. *Ne sis animosus,* "lest you be too venturous."

88. *Fac, &c ,* "see that all this fear of mine go to the winds ;" *i.e.,* prove unfounded. As in v. 69, supply *ut* after *fac.*

89. *Nescio quem,* "some one;" as events proved, Protesilaus himself.

Iniquo, [*in,* neg. and *æquus*] "partial."

90. *Primus,* the superlative of obs. *pris* = *pro,* comp. *prior,* sup. *primus.* So Greek πρὸ, πρότερος, πρότατος, contr. πρῶτος : and in English, *fore, former, foremost,* or *first.*

Troada, Gr. acc. fem. fr. *Trous, Troadis.* Trous was the district in which Troy stood.

92. *Di faciant ne,* "The gods grant that you may not;" *faciant ut* would mean " grant that you may."

Strenuus.—Compare our word *strain ;* "to exert oneself violently." Distinguish *vĕlis* and *vēlis.* *αtrenuus (στοῳ*

93. *Mille,* "a thousand," in round numbers. Homer says 1181 ships sailed against Troy. The number is commonly placed at 1200. *Rates.* Compare English word "raft," here " ships." *Millesima,* "the thousandth," *i.e.,* the last.

94. *Fatigatas,* "wearied" by the oars of the others who had gone before. *Ultima,* " the last." *Ultimus* is the superlative of *ulter,* comp. *ulterior.* Compare Eng. comp. *utter,* super. *uttermost,* or *utmost.*

95. *Novissimus,* "the last," lit. " the newest." The newest thing is necessarily, in many respects, the *latest out.* So we speak of the "*latest news.*" *celerun. (.λελλω)*

97. *Venies,* "when you shall return" home. *Carina,* lit., *keel;* by metonymy, (pars pro toto) *vessel.*

99. *Imago,* " ghost."

101. *Excutior,* [*ex, quatio*] "I am awakened." *Simulacra,* [*similis*] "the phantoms." *Adoro,* [*ad, oro*] "I pray to.'

102. *Thessalis—ara,* " Thessalian altar."

simulacrum (similis)

62 NOTES.

103. *Thura*, fr. *thus*, *thuris;* Gr. θύος. *Sparsa*, fr. *Spargo;* root *spar.* Gr. σπείρω.

104. *Flamma* [Gr. φλέγμα, fr. φλέγω.] *Mero*—see note, Ep. 1, 32.

106. Distinguish *paratĭs* and *paratīs.*

106–109. Three ablatives absolute occur in these lines. *Pelago*, Gr. πέλαγος. This same sea now wears the name of "The Archipelago." *Suam*, because Neptune built Troy's walls. See note Ep. 1, v. 67.

110. *Ruitis, ruo,* Eng. *rush. Redite,* redeo ; fr. *re* and *eo,* with an epenthetic *d. Domos,* Eng. "homes."

111. *Vetantes.*—An elegant reading is *tonantes.*

112. *Subiti casus,* gen. sing., not nom. pl. Translate: "This remarkable (*ista*) delay (of your sailing) is not (the result) of unforeseen chance (but the work) of the deity," *i.e.*, of Neptune.

113. *Adultera.*—Helen.

114. *Inachiæ = Argivæ,* "Grecian ;" from Inachus, an ancient king of the Argives.

115. *Egō.*—Ovid never has the last syllable of *ego* long except in this passage, which has therefore been considered corrupt, and has been altered in various ways. *Revoco,* "call to mind." We use "recall" in exactly the same sense.

116. *Blandaque,* etc.—A line which recalls Byron's beautiful description of the Ægean:

"There mildly dimpling Ocean's cheek," &c.

117. *Claudetur epistola.*—Similarly in English we say, "I must *close* my letter."

118. *Si tibi,* etc., "If you care for me, take care of yourself." A pretty ending to Laodamia's tearful epistle. The other reading, "*Sit tibi cura mei, sit tibi cura tui,*" has not the same force.

EXAMINATION QUESTIONS.

1. Give the dates of the birth and death of Ovid. Where was he born, and where and under what circumstances did he die?
2. Mention some of his contemporaries with their principal works.
3. What civil offices did Ovid hold?
4. Describe his character, and compare it with the character of the age in which he lived.
5. Mention in chronological order the extant poems of Ovid.
6. What circumstances led to his exile?
7. Name the principal writers—Greek and Latin—of Elegiac Verse.
8. How did this species of metre receive its name and in what kinds of composition was it chiefly employed by the Greeks and Romans respectively.
9. To what is the melody of Ovid's Hexameters chiefly owing?
10. What laws regulate the construction of Latin Pentameter Verse? Give a scale of the metre.
11. Give a summary of the principal events during the life of Ovid.
12. Why does Ovid call these letters: *Epistolæ Heroidum?* How many are there of them?
13. Criticise the style of Penelope's letter, its character and poetic merit.

14. Describe from the various allusions in Penelope's letter the condition of affairs in Ulysses' household at Ithaca, at the time when her epistle is represented as having been written. Give this date.

15. What originally was Penelope's name? How did she receive the name Penelope?

16. Write a brief account of the life and νόστος of Ulysses.

17. Describe the geographical position and give the modern names of the several islands which composed Ulysses' kingdom.

18. Give the derivations of *Danais, Priamus, Troja, fallere, viduas, tela* and *pericula.*

19. What remarkable discrepancies in Penelope's letter between the Homeric and Ovidian account of matters *temp.* Trojan war?

20. How many suitors according to Homer had Penelope? Name some of them.

21. Explain the meaning of the phrase: " *Penelopes telum texere,*" " to do and undo"?

22. Give some account of Hector and Patroclus. What is the modern name of the place? Where was Patroclus buried?

23. Why is Nestor called by Attius: " Trisæclisenex"?

24. Derive *altare, barbara, fata, proci, conjux* and *nuper.*

25. Distinguish *inimicus* and *hostis.*

26. *Neleia arva ; Mœnia Phœbi.* Explain.

27. What were the *fata*, retaining which the Trojans should remain invincible? Show how these were overcome.

28. What are the characteristic features of Laodamia's letter. Compare it with Penelope's.

29. Hyginus says Protesilaus was so called because he was

"the first of the people" to land from the Grecian fleet. Narrate the circumstances.

30. *Fama; remus; mandatum; raptus; præceps; nauta; amplexus.* Whence derived?

31. Distinguish frĕta and frēta; vĕlis and vēlis; *sœvus* and *ferus, vultus* and *facies.*

32. Whence did Protesilaus receive the name *Phylacides?*

33. Why is Bacchus called *Bicorniger?*

34. Give the ancient and modern name of the southernmost promontory of Laconia.

35. Distinguish between *gerere* vestes and *gerere* bella; *moenia* and *murus; galea* and *cassis; hostis* and *hospes; redūci* and *redŭci.*

36. Why is Helen called *consors Ledæa gemellis?*

37. What instance of onomatopœia in Laodamia's letter? What of sigmatismus? Cite similar instances in Greek and Latin.

38. Give the derivation of *auspicium, primus, ultimus, sparsus* and *redeo.*

39. What different interpretations of the first two lines and what different readings of the last line of Laodamia's epistle?

40. Draw a map to represent accurately the relative positions of the several places mentioned in the following line:

" *Ilion et Tenedos Simoisque et Xanthus et Ide.*"

www.ingramcontent.com/pod-product-compliance
Lightning Source LLC
Chambersburg PA
CBHW031804090426
42739CB00008B/1162